PINNACLE LEADERSHIP

How to Navigate Change, Move Forward and Reach Your Peak

CHUCK GUMBERT

Throne Publishing Group
220 S Phillips Ave
Sioux Falls, SD
ThronePG.com

PINNACLE
LEADERSHIP

How to Navigate Change,
Move Forward and
Reach Your Peak

CHUCK GUMBERT

THRONE
PUBLISHING GROUP

TESTIMONIALS

"I worked with Chuck at General Electric. I found Chuck to be a strong and decisive leader that made things happen. Chuck never sat on his laurels and nor did he stay satisfied with the status quo. I would recommend Chuck to organizations looking to turn things around."

Stan Gwizdak, CEO

"Chuck does a great job of capturing his leadership recipe in this book. I have witnessed Chuck following these principles in his career. The end results of this process has produced leadership teams that deliver long-term sustainable results…"

Dennis Creekmore, HR Director
Firth Rixson

"Chuck Gumbert learned his craft in one of the greatest leadership training grounds in the world - The United States Navy. In his new book, *Pinnacle Leadership*, he presents the true essence of leadership in a compelling and easy to read style. In clear detail, Chuck identifies the five key elements of leadership, explains each in detail and, more importantly, how they are interrelated. Finally, he shows how to apply them in daily circumstances."

Tom Fricke, Turnaround CEO
Consumer Products, Retail and Restaurants

"I made a small investment in Chuck Gumbert's first book, *Accelerating Performance*. The book, along with Chuck's coaching, has changed not only the way we do business, but our whole outlook on business.

Our revenue was flat, we weren't getting our finished product out on time or on budget, and the finished product wasn't meeting expectations. Chuck worked one-on-one with us and the operation has been cleaned up from bottom to top. Work is done on time; we know what it cost and what the margins are. By straightening out the flow, revenue is up nearly 25% in one year.

Accountability and leadership have been key. The team knows the expectations from job start to finish date. We've improved our overall customer experience. The changes have given us the edge to move upscale in the market, working on far more profitable equipment.

Chuck's business experiences and background helped us set a standard and develop a plan to work toward. I have every confidence that this book will be even better."

Kent McIntyre, President
Bevan Rabell, Inc.

"I met Chuck when he assumed operational responsibility for a company with whom we had a joint venture partnership. At the time of Chuck's arrival we were dismayed at the lack of communication, chronically missed production goals and overall lack of direction.

Through Chuck's leadership, within a very short period of time, communication lines were established followed by detailed operational plans. The whole demeanor of the organization changed from one of doubt and uncertainty to one of purpose. Monthly reports showed steady progress and we achieved our goal of having saleable inventory in stock."

Robert C. Jones
Robert C. Jones Alloys, Inc.

"I first met Chuck Gumbert in the spring of 2014 in Beaumont, Texas and immediately began to feel a sense of leadership from him. We had a lengthy discussion about my goals, management style and strategy going forward. Explaining that I needed a way to expand my comfort zone and empower my safety team to take a more direct approach to managing risk in their respective divisions, Chuck mentored me with his strategy, style and approach. My vision alone was not going to allow me to reach my objectives.

Our company finished 2014 strong by reducing our injury rate by 50% and lowering our vehicle accidents by 30%. Changing my approach to working with my team to accomplish this was a huge breakthrough in my career. Fearing that I would be considered a "micro-manager" kept me up at night, but by working with Mr. Gumbert and following his leadership style I feel like I have become a leader, not just a supervisor."

David Reeder, CSP, Director EHS&C
EMS USA, Inc.

I'D LIKE TO THANK all the mentors, business leaders and employees I've worked with during my 40-year career. This book contains all the learning I've gained from having interacted with each and every one of you.

THIS BOOK IS WHOLLY DEDICATED to my loving wife, Jenny—without your patience and support over the past 35 years, this book could not have been possible.

Success

Accountability

Alignment

Actions

Strategy

Vision

Leadership

TABLE OF
CONTENTS

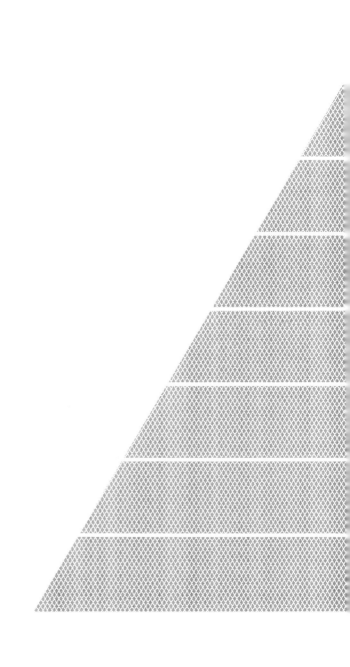

INTRODUCTION

In 2013, Americans started 6,500,000 new businesses. That's approximately 543,000 each and every month. Within 5 years from their grand opening, half of those companies will be done. Within 10 years from startup, only one-third will still be in business. And 15 years out, only a quarter will still be alive.

But just because they are alive, doesn't mean they are performing well.

Think about that: over 6.5 million people stepped out from the crowd with a vision, high hopes and took a big risk that most people never take. Succeed or fail, I admire them for taking a shot. Yet, years later, so few remain in the fight.

Why does failure happen?

How does failure happen?

And more importantly, how can we navigate this ever-changing landscape and continue to move forward?

How can we keep that fire in our hearts burning that compelled us to start our businesses and make them into value-adding machines that bless our families, our communities and us?

I am absolutely convinced that success is the result of very simple principles. These principles are far from easy, but they are simple—principles that must be executed with an attitude of never ending improvement and a spirit of relentless discipline.

Anyone can execute them—*you* can execute them.

During my career, I have had the opportunity to work with corporations that were generating anywhere from $2.5 - 175M in annual revenue. Some of those organizations were performing well, while many fell short of expectations. The approach discussed in this book provides a proven "Back to Basics" methodology that can work with any business, large or small, where the leader is ready and willing to take action and *Move Forward*. By applying these principles, you too will see dramatic changes in revenue and profitability.

I wrote this book to be a plan of action for you. Not just to talk theories and stories, but to give you the facts and the simple truths that will propel your organization toward growth. You will find the chapters are straight forward and to the point. We'll get right into it. At the end of each chapter there are questions—hard questions that are meant to get you into action.

I hope you take this book, read it, re-read it and scribble it with notes, ideas and action plans. That's how it is designed to function. And if you work the plan, the plan will work for you. You will *Navigate Change* and *Move Forward*. And you will get out what you put into it.

I appreciate you reading my introduction—Thank You. Now, let's get started.

LEADERSHIP

Success

_____

Accountability

_____

Alignment

_____

Actions

_____

Strategy

_____

Vision

_____

Leadership

> "A LEADER IS ONE WHO **KNOWS** THE WAY, **GOES** THE WAY AND **SHOWS** THE WAY."

John Maxwell

CHAPTER 1

Allow me to start with a question: What stands as the beginning of your successful business?

The answer is leadership.

Who is responsible for the leadership of your business?

You.

WHO IS RESPONSIBLE FOR THE LEADERSHIP OF YOUR BUSINESS?

YOU.

Leadership is the genesis from which all the successes and failures of a business come. Any organization stands and falls by its leaders, and every leader must know their business starts with one person. You. To advance as a company, someone, the leader, must step up and present him or herself as the go-to person—the one supplying direction, providing accountability, and ultimately moving the business, as a whole, forward.

In order for your people to see you as their leader, it's your responsibility and opportunity to step up and lead.

The leader sets the pace. They are the ones who build a vision, work with the organization on developing a strategy of action, and make sure that actions are aligned and executed in cohesion with the vision.

Without strong leadership, how will a business be held accountable? Employees will never understand where they are *going* with their work if their leader does not introduce a goal and make that goal clear across the entire business. Behind the goals and strategies of every company there must be a leader sorting out the logistics: How much time, working capital and effort is this going to take? What resources do we have available? Who are our customers? What profit will this bring? No one else has the authority or the vantage point to construct big-picture plans, and ensure their execution like leaders do.

Leaders initiate the change needed in their corporate culture by being the first to exemplify it. And this is more than just an area of change; it's a whole new way of operation.

Though no leader is perfect, some are better than others. In my experience, the men and women who grasp leadership best are those who are dedicated to improving who *they* are as people, as much as they are dedicated to the success of their business. Here are four fundamental characteristics of great leaders:

1. Mentoring

The best kinds of leaders are mentors. Instructing your employees with an iron fist won't better them as individuals or employees. However, being a mentor to those you lead in your company will catalyze

THE BEST KINDS OF LEADERS ARE MENTORS.

their growth into positive people and productive contributors. This kind of mentorship usually requires instruction: take the time to invest in your employees by instructing them in their work and even in their lives. Often times they have more potential than they realize. Leaders are in a unique position to help employees better themselves. Leaders develop others.

Ask your employees where *they* want to be in 5 years. And I'm talking about their personal lives. Talk to them about their goals and their strategies to get there. Much like their business strategies, leaders can help individuals develop a strategy of actions to execute, in order to reach their goals in life.

2. Learning

You don't know everything. I don't know everything. However, I learn something new every day that strengthens my leadership. This is not only because I spend lots of my time working out "on the floor," or dealing with customers—though these are valuable parts of leadership too—but because I am dedicated to developing myself in all areas of life. My development as a person is, in part, due to the many indirect mentors that have taught me so much over the years. I am constantly updating my skill-set by learning from others. This includes not only direct interaction, but also learning through books, seminars and outside coursework. And the best kinds of leaders not only capitalize on the wisdom of others to become widely functional people; they also share that wisdom with their teams.

3. Listening

I think a common perception of leaders is that they are primarily instructors or enforcers. Indeed, leaders must be these things. But they also need to be people who listen—listen to outside sources, listen to new ideas, listen to employees. It comes down to what I said above: leaders don't know everything, and the primary way you learn is by listening. In my experience, I learn more by walking through an operation and talking to employees than I do from sitting in most staff meetings. In staff meetings everyone tends to be guarded and quiet—reluctant to share problems or point out behaviors or areas that need correction in the business. But engaging and *listening* to employees helps me to understand how I can lead them better. This means *really* listening to what they have to say. You simply can't do this kind of leading from inside an office.

4. Futuristic

If I am flying from Los Angeles to Minneapolis, my route will be simple and direct—unless weather or crosswinds blow me off track to the east or west. When this happens, I am no longer flying directly towards Minneapolis; I will have to make the necessary course adjustments to get back on the right track. Leaders need to know that winds of change will surely knock them off course, but that shouldn't stop them from achieving their goals. They should adjust, adapt and overcome the obstacles. Make the right course adjustments and tweaks to get your business heading the direction it needs to be. This is how leaders keep the pace. Their eyes are always on the future and looking for ways to do things better.

I know many business leaders who have great ideas but fail to execute those ideas to their fullest potential. This is no shock; when an idea is thwarted, it is tempting to simply resort to a new idea or take a new course. But I believe good leaders set an achievable course for their business and stick to that course until they reach their goals. Of course, unexpected winds will catch you off guard, but sticking to your plans (short-term *and* long-term) is crucial to your big-picture success.

Never forget, you are the genesis of your business. Everything that your business produces and accomplishes begins and ends with you and no one else. Only when you have truly accepted this principle and embraced the process of leadership growth will it begin to transform how you lead yourself, your household and ultimately your business. Having discussed some of the most important characteristics of leaders, I am confident that you have already begun to grow as one—and as a person. Use your unique station to mentor, learn, listen, and orchestrate the production of your business to new degrees of achievement. It all begins and ends with leadership.

WHAT IS HOLDING YOU BACK FROM BECOMING A BETTER LEADER?

Question

2

HOW WOULD THE WISEST PERSON YOU KNOW RESPOND TO YOUR ANSWERS TO QUESTION NUMBER ONE?

Question

3

WHAT NEEDS TO BE ELIMINATED FROM YOUR LIFE IN ORDER FOR YOU TO BECOME BETTER?

Question

4

WHAT NEEDS TO BE ADDED IN ORDER FOR YOU TO BECOME BETTER?

WHAT WOULD BE SOME OF THE RESULTS IN YOUR ORGANIZATION AND IN YOUR LIFE IF YOU WERE A BETTER LEADER?

CHAPTER 2
VISION

Success

Accountability

Alignment

Actions

Strategy

Vision

Leadership

"**VISION** HAS NO BOUNDARIES AND KNOWS NO LIMITS. OUR **VISION** IS WHAT WE BECOME IN LIFE."

Tony Dungy

CHAPTER 2

"Where are we going?"

This is the most significant question a business can ask itself. And it demands an answer.

Every business must ask this question before it goes anywhere.

In the last chapter we discussed the importance of leadership within your business; now we will turn to see how crucial the vision of that leadership is. I often visit businesses and ask the staff and employees this very question: *Where are you going?* I'm sad to say that nine times out of ten they have no answer. They don't know. To compound the issue, many of these business leaders cannot relay to me where their business is going in exact terms. Usually they are more concerned with a general sense of growth—meeting deadlines and making enough profit. But in this chapter, we will see that if your business does not know precisely where it's going, it will never go where you want it to.

Simply put, to have a *vision* is to answer, *where are we going, and why?* Only when a business can answer these questions will it have a definite *vision* or purpose—a set path and destination. As we have

SIMPLY PUT, TO HAVE A *VISION* IS TO ANSWER, *WHERE ARE WE GOING,* AND *WHY?*

witnessed, businesses start with leaders. In the same way, *visions* start with leaders who courageously chart the course for where the business is to go. It is the leader's primary responsibility to establish that *vision* and consistently communicate it to the rest of the organization.

I encourage business leaders to seek input and converse with leadership teams or advisory groups when creating their *vision*; go to other leaders and people of power to help you refine your ideas. Consolidate your resources and relations to present the best possible direction for your business. This defines where you are going and empowers you to boldly tell your organization and the world *where you are going!*

Perhaps it will be helpful to contrast a leader who has *no* definite *vision* with one who does.

A leader without a *vision* is what I call an "Idea Guy." Idea Guys are usually entrepreneurs who have big dreams in their heads, but no ability to sit down and formulate them into reality. If you are unable to formulate your ideas, you will never be able to adequately communicate your ideas. And an idea that can't be communicated will never be executed. Consequently, this only leads to frustration. Either the leader is unable to communicate the idea to the rest of the team, or he/she assumes the team understands the idea when, in reality, they don't. Either way, it leaves the leader in a frustrated position—all because they couldn't translate their ideas into words.

Not only does this failure frustrate leaders; it also leads to confusion among the rest of the organization. If employees don't clearly understand the direction of the business (communicated to them by the leader), then their task becomes somewhat ambiguous. People begin to work towards subjective goals that they think make the most sense, which provokes wrong behavior and discord in the work environment. This kind of an environment only engenders chaos within the business. Employees become frustrated that their work seems detached from the others, which brings about all kinds of conflicts. And if leaders have no vision to address these conflicts, they will remain unresolved. If there is no initial direction to refer back to, workers will not know if they are on track or that they have left it. In the worst of cases, this ends with frustrated businesses losing highly talented and extremely valuable people. Really good people are looking for direction and solid leaders, not a workplace of confusion and chaos.

In some instances Idea Guys simply have issues committing to one *vision*.

They set a direction for their business and communicate it well, but change their mind about the *vision* or direction before reaching it. This also triggers business frustration: how can your team complete their mission if the mission is always changing? If you find yourself needing to alter your vision a few months after introducing it, perhaps that idea wasn't thought out well enough to begin with.

On the other hand, leaders who have a finely tuned *vision* know to formulate, write down, and document that *vision* for it to be successfully implemented into the business. It has been cultivated and refined to a functional level. Further, and most importantly, the vision is consistently communicated. Great leaders are committed to making their vision crystal-clear to everyone—from their leadership teams to the custodians. Rather than chaos, this communication builds camaraderie in your business. Employees know exactly where they are being led, and thus, they can work together to reach that end—generating harmony and profit, not frustration. This builds structure and teamwork within your business. A communicated vision puts leaders and workers on the same page. Workers no longer feel like wandering generalities, as it were, but employees on a mission, who are all dedicated to one mutual cause: the *vision.*

If you are a CEO or leader of your company without a vision, here are three crucial steps you can take to develop one:

1. Ask yourself, "Why did I start this business in the first place?"

ASK YOURSELF, "WHY DID I START THIS BUSINESS IN THE FIRST PLACE?"

Go back to the start—the genesis. There is a reason you created (or stepped into) this business. Perhaps you wanted to help people, solve some problem, make money or cultivate an idea. No matter, a *vision* is the very reason any business exists. Think back to the beginning and remember what moved you to start this endeavor in the first place. Why did you think this was a good idea? Answering this will help you bring that *vision* back into focus to adjust and execute in your business.

2. Receive feedback

Once you have refocused this vision, go to your leadership teams, advisors, family members, and other people you trust for feedback. Formulate your vision, communicate it to them, and listen to what they have to say. On the one hand, this process allows you to refine the vision; on the other hand, it simultaneously acclimates the mindset of your business. Talk about the vision you're creating every day. Let it saturate you and your employees' thoughts.

3. Present the picture of where you're going

You've gone back to your initial motivation for creating the business; you've communicated and bounced that *vision* off others for feedback; now, your final step is to clearly establish and communicate that vision to set the direction of the business—not only the direction you're heading together, but the destination you're striving towards as well. On the whole, this is a process of remembering, refining, and reinforcing the vision for your business and to set your course…every day!

This concept is not incredibly profound. However, if you—as the leader—do not take these steps, your business will never really know where it is *going*, or what it is *doing*. The rest of this book builds on top of a firm and vivid *vision*. So, take the time to establish one you believe in—for your success as a leader, and the success of your business as a whole. Use your unique position as leader to set the direction. No one else can make this call. Be bold and courageous and build your future!

Question

1

CAN YOU ANSWER THE QUESTION "WHERE ARE WE GOING" IN ONE OR TWO SENTENCES?

Question

2

DOES YOUR TEAM KNOW YOUR VISION? TO WHAT DEGREE OF CLARITY?

HOW WOULD YOUR DAY-TO-DAY WORK CHANGE IF YOU HAD A CLEAR VISION THAT WAS EXHILARATING TO YOU?

Question

4

HOW MUCH TIME ARE YOU GOING TO DEDICATE TO CREATING A CLEAR VISION?

What is one action you are going to implement as a result of reading this chapter?

CHAPTER 3
STRATEGY

Success

Accountability

Alignment

Actions

Strategy

Vision

Leadership

"WHATEVER YOU CAN DO, OR DREAM YOU CAN DO, BEGIN IT. BOLDNESS HAS GENIUS, POWER, AND MAGIC IN IT. **BEGIN IT NOW.**"

William Hutchinson Murray

CHAPTER 3

In the last chapter, I established that the most important question a business can ask itself is, "Where are we going?" And, as we have seen, only a defined Vision for that business can answer such a question. In this chapter, we will face the second most important question: "What's the plan?" A business with a suitable Vision must proceed to develop a suitable *Strategy* in order to attain that Vision. For, even a great Vision that does not mature into a Strategy is of no use; establishing a Strategy is the next fundamental step to reaching that overarching Vision for your organization or business.

If the Vision of your business is its purpose, your Strategy is simply the path you plan to take to fulfill that objective. It is like a road map. If I am on a trip from Los Angeles to Sacramento, then Sacramento is my objective; the road map contains my Strategy.

Strategy is the action plan you develop to achieve your Vision. It really is quite simple—but I have seen too many businesses that try to survive and grow without a defined Strategy, and frankly, it's painful and costly. To help emphasize the importance of a solidified Strategy, I will discuss a few indicators of these businesses that do not have a solid Strategy, and the consequences that follow.

Just as a lack of Vision results in chaos and inner turmoil within a business, the lack of Strategy engenders confusion about the actual direction and intentions of the company. Often times, companies unknowingly comprise a whole list of actions or expectations that do not even match up with each other, leaving workers confused, and rendering the business as a whole rather chaotic. Similarly, a business without a defined Strategy will routinely change its direction—giving rise to a sort of company "flavor of the month" mentality. One day "We are going to do X"; a few days later "We are going to do Y." While this is clearly a simple example, the same mentality will make its way into the operations group, marketing team, sales team and everywhere else if there is no set Strategy from which to gauge every action.

A business with no Strategy has no baseline. They are ultimately unable to identify what they are going to do, and how they plan to do it. They are a ship without a rudder, wandering aimlessly at sea without a defined direction.

On the other hand, a business *with* an established Strategy has a clear direction. They are laser-focused and know where they are going. In the last chapter we discussed the impacts of a clear Vision; a Strategy produces many of the same results. It sets the appropriate direction, thus reducing chaos and frustration while building a mentality that guides every decision made within the business.

A BUSINESS WITH AN ESTABLISHED STRATEGY HAS A CLEAR DIRECTION. THEY ARE LASER-FOCUSED AND KNOW WHERE THEY ARE GOING.

A Strategy, in some sense, is a standard by which every decision can be judged. If any decision deviates from the Strategy of your business, that decision will potentially compromise attainment of the Vision. This is why it is absolutely crucial for you—as the leader—to establish a Strategy for your whole organization that sets the direction. Every meeting you sit in and every document you look through should tie back to your Strategy in a definite way. This will work again and again to keep your business on the same page, and decrease the number of times you're potentially thrown off course—all because you and your team know and fully understand the Strategy.

If you are reading this and realize that your business does not have a clear Strategy, then here are some steps you can take to begin to establish one. Keep in mind, this may seem like a daunting task, but I want to encourage you—just the mere act of deciding to create a Strategy and stick with it will sharpen your mind, quicken your step and spark a flame inside you that will automatically begin to improve your organization's productivity. You absolutely can do this - I know it; and you will believe it once you begin. Keep in mind the quote at the beginning of this chapter. Just deciding will foster new ideas in your mind that will, without question, give you *all* the ideas you need to create a defined Strategy for your business that will give you and your team the motivation to move forward.

1. Establish 4-6 Primary Directives

To begin, set 4-6 primary directives that set the tone for the entire remaining portion of your Strategy. Don't be too specific here: these are meant to be high-level and overarching key elements that you will break down into smaller, specific steps later on. For now, make sure these directives set a definite tone—ones that you want to permeate and support your entire Strategy and attainment of the Vision. I have found that having more than 6 primary directives is too many. If you find yourself with more, take some time to refine them—simplify and skim them down. If everything is important, then nothing will *really* be important. I call these *primary* directives for a reason; they are not meant to be exhaustive or specific, but rather high-level enough for the specifics to fit within and support.

2. Break Down Your Directives

Once you have identified 4-6 overarching directives, you will be able to break them down into supporting sub-directives or tactical plans. Begin to make an outline of the directives, but make sure every aspect fits in and supports one primary directive. For example, perhaps your business wants to be the *number one* car dealer in Kansas. If this is a primary directive, you need to break that down into more attainable specifics. What make/model of cars will you sell? Will you sell higher end or lower end cars? How/where will you market your business? This is what it means to break down your directives.

3. Communicate It

Now we need to communicate these directives. Again, this is similar to your Vision; make the Strategy known to everyone in the business. Begin to explain how it is broken down and why you've broken it down in such a way. Make sure that everybody understands what it is they are going to do, and that they understand the particular role they play in the execution of the Strategy. A Strategy that is not communicated is of no use to you.

Communicate it, keep it simple and follow through.

I want you to find a Strategy that you are confident in and communicate it with boldness and audacity. Thus, I want you to develop a Strategy that is well defined and appropriate for your organization. Like we discussed in chapter two, utilize your position as a leader, but also utilize and engage your leadership team. Talk this through with them and take the time to establish a clear, defined and purposeful Strategy with their input. If you cannot communicate your Strategy clearly, then it probably isn't a very good Strategy. So take the time to ask yourself the hard questions: "Will the key elements of this Strategy support our primary directive?" "Are we doing this because it will lead to fulfillment of the Vision?"

As the leader, you need to be relatively flexible while you are formulating the Strategy. You and your team may need some time to do the research required to give you enough information to establish your primary directives. For example, if you hope to expand your sales target, you'll need to conduct some demographic, product and competitor research. In my experience, the main cause for a Strategy failure is simply that it wasn't well thought out. Take the time you need. Plans may go out the window when you begin to execute, but planning is simply indispensable. You will be glad you did—and even more importantly, your team will deeply respect you for taking time to do this.

You should be able to pin down your 4-6 primary directives and a few sub points within a couple of weeks. In this time period, make sure you can work without being distracted; dedicate the resources and facilitate sessions for your team to brainstorm and chew through thoughts. Set a deadline if you need to.

The more focused you can be, the more defined the Strategy, the more confident you can be that it will function just as you planned. And the more confidence you have, the more

KEEP IN MIND THAT HOPE IS NOT A STRATEGY.

committed your team will be to that Strategy. When teams and leaders truly believe they have a well thought out and defined Strategy, they will easily commit and readily sign up for it.

Keep in mind that *Hope* is not a Strategy. Do not simply hope the Strategy works; invest the necessary time, research, and brainstorming to build a

Strategy that you and your team are *convinced* will work.

I am absolutely convinced that a good Strategy will renovate your business, your attitude and set the stage for success. When your team knows and understands exactly what their objective is, you can cease to micromanage every aspect of your organization, and instead, watch it perform the way your Strategy planned. As a leader, you will be free to coach your business, not hold it together by yourself. Who knows, maybe you can even take a couple days a week off!

Whatever the end result is for you, I can tell you this: Creating your Strategy will require time, attention and the hardest labor in the world - *thinking*. But if you put a lot of energy into this, you are going to reap a harvest that includes higher profitability, highly satisfied customers, happier employees and results that will be envied by your competitors.

ON A SCALE FROM 1-10, 10 BEING TOTALLY CLEAR, HOW WOULD YOU RATE THE CLARITY OF YOUR STRATEGIC PLAN FOR YOUR ORGANIZATION?

Question

2

WHAT IS ONE ACTION YOU CAN IMPLEMENT TO IMPROVE ON YOUR STRATEGY?

WHAT IS THE BIGGEST ROADBLOCK WHEN CLARIFYING YOUR STRATEGY?

HOW MUCH BETTER DO YOU THINK YOUR LEADERSHIP TEAM WOULD PERFORM WITH A CLEAR STRATEGY, AND WHY?

WHEN WAS A TIME WHEN YOU FELT LIKE YOU HAD A CLEAR STRATEGY? WHAT WERE THE RESULTS?

CHAPTER 4
ACTIONS

Success

Accountability

Alignment

Actions

Strategy

Vision

Leadership

> "**FAR BETTER IS IT TO DARE MIGHTY THINGS**, TO WIN GLORIOUS TRIUMPHS, EVEN THOUGH CHECKERED BY FAILURE..."

Theodore Roosevelt

CHAPTER 4

Just as a vision without a congruent strategy is useless, so too is strategy without actions. Through the process of time, your strategy could become nothing more than a distant memory and fleeting moment of motivation. Expect and anticipate your motivation level and commitment to be tested. Emotions come and go—alter and change just as the weather—so this is why having a clear set of actions will greatly help you remain persistent through the challenges.

In the last chapter, I discussed the vitality of a strong strategy for your business. It may go without saying, but the whole purpose of a strategy is to initiate and ensure action that moves your business forward. So in this chapter, we will begin to move from the realm of the hypothetical to the practical—from the dream to the everyday work required to execute your strategy. As we have already discussed, this is a process of breaking down your strategy to specific actionable pieces. Such specificity requires more: more discussion, more decisiveness, more effort and more of you.

This is the chapter that separates the winners from the wanna-be's. You will be required to dig deep, to think in ways you may not have thought and stretch your comfort-zone to a level that it has not been before.

My aim here is to empower you as a business leader to begin breaking down your strategy into definite, actionable pieces. There is no room for doubt anymore. Begin by selecting one of your Primary Directives and ask yourself:

"How are we going to accomplish this?"

Asking "how" is the first step to breaking that element down into very specific, detailed tactical plans. Be specific to the point that every part of the organization will know exactly what they must do to accomplish this element of the strategy. Operations, sales and marketing, finance, IT, materials, HR—every part of the business should be able to see their role in supporting this strategic element. By the time you have broken down your

IMAGINE THE CHANGE IN YOUR COMPANY'S CULTURE WHEN EVERYONE KNOWS THE DIRECTION THE COMPANY IS MOVING, THE ACTION PLAN TO GET THERE AND THEIR SPECIFIC ROLE IN THIS VISION.

entire strategy, your entire organization will know precisely what to do and how their day-to-day actions are a part of something much bigger than themselves.

Imagine the change in your company's culture when everyone knows the direction the company is moving, the action plan to get there and their specific role in this vision. This is what puts the *force* in your workforce.

SMART Goals

Action plans should be smart in character. By this, I mean they need to be specific, measurable, attainable, relevant, and timely. This is a great way of measuring ever action plan you make. Further, all action plans should be tied very closely to your overall strategy. If, while breaking down one Primary Directive, you realize some action no longer supports the vision of your organization, that action is no longer smart—cut it out. Only break down elements of your strategy to the points to which they need to be broken down. Clarity and effectiveness are the aims here, not excess. Sophistication resides in simplicity.

It is no surprise that this too is an area where many organizations fail. I have talked about "Idea Guys" in recent chapters—the kind of business leaders who develop great and grand visions for their organizations, but fail to follow them through. These leaders do not see their dreams come to full fruition because they do not commit to specific action plans for their organization to execute properly. Commitment on any level is challenging; it is no different here.

That is why I encourage businesses leaders to find accountability for their action plans. Find someone—a business consultant, a coach, etc.—who will directly ask you if you are following through with the actions you've said you would take. However, commitment is a transition from the hope of success, to the pursuit of success. Rather than merely *wanting* a certain gain, you begin to *attain* a certain gain—and that is the very end we are after.

SWOT Analysis

One helpful way of measuring the action-effectiveness of your strategy is to perform a SWOT analysis. A SWOT analysis is a list (written down) of your Strengths, Weakness, Opportunities, and Threats. The purpose of creating this list is to uncover an accurate picture of where you are currently standing as a business. Many business leaders would much rather see where they are trying to go than where they currently are; however, you will never *Move Forward*—towards your objectives—if you don't know where your business stands now.

This information is often times undesirable—revealing the failures and problems in your business; but, I promise you, it will prove to be invaluable, and absolutely crucial for understanding what exactly you need to do to grow.

For example, if you want to grow 20%, how are you going to do that? Start to weigh your options. How can you get more business out of current customers, or seek new customers from either new or local areas? Could you develop new marketing channels on the Internet—Facebook, Twitter, blog, etc? Could you sign up with a distributor to produce more products, or should you develop new products yourself? In the end, this is all a matter of brainstorming—and it is this kind of brainstorming from which you will extract those very specific action plans that can move you towards growing your business 20%, or more.

One primary reason many businesses fail to transition from strategy to action is they simply get distracted. If you are the owner of a hardware store, and another hardware store opens up down the street, don't instantly give up or feel the need to change your vision. You may, it's true, need to adjust and alter some action plans, but your objectives remain the same. Some leaders may find it hard to commit to their own action plans in circumstances like these. Again, this is why accountability is absolutely crucial. Find people who will keep you committed to the plans you've measured out and set before the business. Without accountability it is too easy to make excuses and get off track—too easy to get distracted from your action plans. With that being said, I press in to encourage, support and help my clients keep moving forward. I have yet to hear from anyone who regretted being held accountable.

In fact, I am eager to receive your emails, asking for help with accountability; I intend to be here for you, and I want to see your strategies transform into actions.

As you are breaking down your Primary Directives into more specific steps, remember that you must actually commit to the action plans you make. They are not merely potential options for how to proceed; they are the force with which your business is going to move forward. For some people, this requires an entire shift in thought; it is no longer a matter of dreaming, but of doing.

IT IS NO LONGER A MATTER OF DREAMING, BUT OF DOING.

You must know that well developed visions, strategies, and action plans are of course easier to commit to than insubstantial ones. So take the time and do the brainstorming necessary to break down your strategy into smart, specific action plans that you know your business will be able to commit to as a whole. This is "want to" vs. "will do." This is where all your planning from previous chapters starts to work itself out in your business. Get out there and take some action. In the words of the great Thomas Jefferson: "Do you want to know who you are? Don't ask. Act! Action will delineate and define you."

WHAT ARE THE MOST IMPORTANT ACTIONS YOU NEED TO BE EXECUTING EVERY SINGLE DAY?

Question

2

Do you feel like you know exactly what you need to get done on a day-to-day basis?

DO YOU THINK YOUR KEY LEADERS KNOW EXACTLY WHAT THEY NEED TO GET DONE ON A DAY-TO-DAY BASIS?

Question

4

WHEN IS THE LAST TIME YOU DID A SWOT ANALYSIS ON YOUR ORGANIZATION?

WHAT ARE THE GREATEST STRENGTHS (NAME TWO OR THREE) AND BIGGEST WEAKNESSES (TWO OR THREE) IN YOUR ORGANIZATION TODAY?

CHAPTER 5
ALIGNMENT

Success

Accountability

Alignment

Actions

Strategy

Vision

Leadership

"You **PERFORM BETTER** WHEN YOUR THOUGHTS, FEELINGS, EMOTIONS, GOALS, AND VALUES ARE IN **BALANCE**."

Brian Tracy

CHAPTER 5

With a vivid vision, a fully developed strategy, and enough specific actions plans to execute that strategy, your next step as a business leader is to focus on *alignment*. This means getting your teams on board with your vision, strategy, and action plans. To see the manifestations of these three categories, you need a team who backs them as much as you do—and that means your business needs a comprehensive sense of unity; you need alignment.

TO HAVE ALIGNMENT MEANS TO HAVE EVERYONE WITHIN YOUR ORGANIZATION— BOTH PERSONALLY AND DEPARTMENTALLY—MOVING IN THE SAME DIRECTION

Most basically, to have alignment means to have everyone within your organization— both personally and departmentally—moving in the same direction. Each goal and every objective the business sets and meets are aligned.

Here is a helpful metaphor: all of the *parts* of an arrow—head, shaft, and fletching—point in the same direction. The parts work together to ensure the arrow will fly in a single direction. In the same way, all of the parts of your organization must point in one direction for it to move in the course you want it to. All of the parts, the teams, of your organization must be aligned. If half of your business backs your vision, and the other half is skeptical (or merely uninformed about that vision), do you think that vision will ever come to fruition? Not likely. Let's take a look, then, at some of the positive effects of alignment within your organization.

With Alignment…

Firstly, your progression towards executing the strategy and obtaining the vision is going to be much faster when alignment is present. When your teams start on the same page, and move in the same direction from the word "Go," meeting these goals will not only be possible, it will be a smoother and less painful process for everyone. One helpful way to think about alignment is to consider trajectory. If your business has one collective *trajectory*, a single direction, chances are your business has its alignment in place.

Similarly, alignment eliminates and alleviates conflict within the organization. We have discussed this in recent chapters, but you can be sure that a business with much conflict does *not* have alignment between its functioning teams and members. Because a cohesive alignment reduces conflict, it consequently keeps employees around longer. This, of course, allows you to generate products and get them to the market faster.

Alignment has the ability to bolster your employee's pride of ownership in their work: they feel they are a part of a broader team, and they can see their role in that team as significant. For the CEO, this simplifies your work (and life). If your business is a well oiled, functioning machine, you no longer have to perform maintenance on it all the time (micromanaging). Now, rather than constantly directing and monitoring the functions of the business, you can step back and watch it execute properly, investing your time and energies more efficiently. All because the business has alignment!

Take, for example, how alignment functions in the vehicle you drive. A vehicle with perfect alignment will continue to drive in a strait line even when you take both hands off the wheel (I am not suggesting you try this). However, most of us know what it's like to drive a vehicle with an alignment that is simply off. It either wants to steer itself over to the left or the right, if you take your hands *off* the wheel for even a second.

When running your business, you should not always have to keep both hands on the wheel, as it were; the alignment of your organization should be such that it can continue moving in one singular direction without your constant correction. This is the power of alignment. Organizations with *off* alignment usually leave their original strategy and veer over to a different one, because the task of constantly correcting the direction is too overwhelming. Or, all too often, they will revert to *"making the month,"* which is no strategy at all.

Making Alignment Happen

Let's say you just finished a meeting with your leadership team. In that meeting you finalized the vision, strategy, and action plans for your organization for the next few years (great!). Your next step is to build and ensure alignment throughout every department! Here are some practical ways you can do just that:

To begin, make sure the action plans you've developed all work *together*. When communicating them to your business, you must first be certain they are aligned in such a way that those actions will actually move your business towards its objective. Thus, alignment isn't only something that happens *after* you make your plans, but something that must be kept in mind *while* you're making plans—while you're brainstorming. If your business is going to have alignment, you need to develop action plans that work together, and involve your whole business, not just one department. This kind of planning will maintain alignment while you execute those actions, preventing parts or teams from deviating from their responsibilities or redundant actions.

This is also a good place to implement *incentive programs* within the business. Getting employees on board with the broader goal of the organization can be tricky; often times, people would rather stick to the success of their own department and forget about the rest. However, I have found that a good incentive is often enough to bring employees from a mere departmental commitment, to one that cares equally as much for the company as a whole. Know your employees; work with them as they work with you.

Next, make sure you can track how you're doing in accordance with your goals and objectives. Being able to see the success or failure of an objective will tell you if that objective is aligned with the greater vision of the business. Make sure you have specific dates by which you plan to meet specific objectives. Without a system that allows you to track how your action plans are functioning, it will be much harder to see whether or not those actions are continually parallel with your original vision—especially for organizations with many different departments.

Imagine you walk into a department store that's pushing a new product. You approach a sales clerk at the counter and, after a few questions concerning that product, realize she doesn't appear to care about it on a personal level *at all.* In fact, she tells you that though the store launched the campaign last week, they were not really prepared and no longer have that product in store. I'm sure we've all had an experience like this one.

What happened?

Simply put, the goals of the store weren't aligned. Perhaps someone dropped the ball on educating the sales clerk adequately; or maybe someone on the supply chain team didn't make sure the store would have that product this campaign was pushing. Either way, there are missing pieces; something wasn't aligned along the way. This is a clear sign that a business has lost its ability to move forward in any significant way. Conflicting goals— between teams, employees, etc.—cause a sort of inner-organizational tug-of-war that either immobilizes productivity, or drives the business from its initial trajectory.

I want you to be able to avoid this kind of immobilization. And I want your business to find a steady alignment! As you begin to consider alignment, remember that it has everything to do with your initial goals, and with the communication of those goals. If it seems to you, as a leader, that

DON'T BE AFRAID TO LOOK BACK.

your business has no alignment, the problem likely stems from a plan that wasn't developed well in the past—or a good plan that wasn't communicated enough. So, don't be afraid to look back. Ask yourself often if your action plans are aligned with the overarching goal of your organization. And, as always, simply take the time to watch your action plans work themselves out day-to-day. When the functions of your business move in different directions, you will never have alignment. However, I hope this chapter has served to show you the necessity of an appropriate alignment in your business, and, of course, the numerous advantages it will bring.

Question

1

WHAT IS THE BIGGEST CONCEPT THAT JUMPED OUT AT YOU IN THIS CHAPTER?

Question

2

ON A SCALE OF 1-10, 10 BEING TOTAL ALIGNMENT IN ALL DEPARTMENTS, WHAT WOULD YOU RATE YOUR ORGANIZATION'S ALIGNMENT TODAY?

WHERE IN YOUR ORGANIZATION IS ALIGNMENT CREATING THE BIGGEST PROBLEMS?

Question

4

What would be the biggest action you could take to help your organization become more aligned?

WHAT IS THE #1 ACTION YOU WILL IMPLEMENT AS A RESULT OF THIS CHAPTER, AND WHY?

CHAPTER 6
ACCOUNTABILITY

Success

Accountability

Alignment

Actions

Strategy

Vision

Leadership

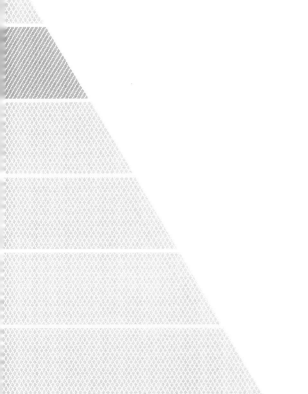

"ACCOUNTABILITY BREEDS RESPONSE-ABILITY."

Stephen Covey

CHAPTER 6

The next concept I'd like to turn your attention towards is similar to, but not synonymous with alignment: namely, *accountability*. We are all familiar, in some ways, with it—and I don't intend to redefine how you think of it here. Rather, in this chapter I hope to discuss the simple role of accountability in reaching your vision, and urge you, as the leader, to establish it in your organization.

Nevertheless, it will again be helpful to start with a simple definition. Accountability is the means by which you assure that everyone is doing what he or she is supposed to do.

ACCOUNTABILITY IS THE MEANS BY WHICH YOU ASSURE THAT EVERYONE IS DOING WHAT HE OR SHE IS SUPPOSED TO DO.

To hold anyone accountable is to hold them to a standard—a quota, expectation, promise—that they are to meet or fulfill. Like the other facets of this book, accountability is contingent upon clear communication throughout your organization. And it will, if communicated, ensure that your action plans successfully execute your strategy, in order to ultimately fulfill your vision. Let's take a closer look at the value of accountability in your business.

Accountability provides a structure in which you and your business can operate—a sort of paradigm that allows for your employees to know what is expected of them. Because accountability sets a standard in your business, it helps guide and *align* its everyday executions.

Currently, it seems widespread that being "held accountable" is a negative idea, something that suggests failure. However, accountability is neutral in itself, and can (should) be used to point out both the successes and shortcomings of your business. If Sally submits a lousy report a day late, she may need correction; if Sally submits an exceptional report a day early, she deserves a word of praise. Both are tied in to holding her accountable to the report she was originally assigned to do. Because Sally is *expected* to submit a good report on time by her leaders or boss, she is being held accountable.

It will be helpful to break this down further. Above I spoke of a "standard" that accountability sets. I have found that this standard should usually consist of three particular categories:

1. The quality of the end result
2. A specific timeline
3. The attitude with which the work is done

As leader, it is absolutely *crucial* for you to set the expectation for all three of these categories. If you do not, your organization will never know what they are being held accountable to, or they will set their own subjective standards. As we discussed last chapter, a business will never move forward in one singular direction if its workers are not of one accord. Harmony of purpose is necessary for a business to achieve its purpose and maintain alignment. Thus, workers need to know precisely what is expected of them—and that means you need to set the expectations.

Setting expectations in your business is not a passive thing. As the leader, it is equally important that you embody those standards in your own work. If one of your categories of accountability is *timeline*, you must be a timely leader. That means showing up to meetings on time, finishing assignments by the *time* you said you would, etc. This is a vital part of communicating expectations to your business—*the business sees you setting them every day.* Take a firm stand and fulfill your goal as leader, for you truly are leading the whole organization in a direction with your everyday actions.

Verbal communication of expectations is perhaps the simplest way to develop accountability in your business. Employees will know what they are *supposed to do* when you (or other leaders) have told them. This means making it crystal clear what is expected of the end result, what the timeline of the work is, and what attitude workers must exhibit. Make it plain.

Of course, relaying to your business *what* they are to do does not ensure that it *will* be accomplished, but it is a necessary step. Fortunately, communicating what is expected in the business often simply means explaining the vision, strategy, and action plans you have already developed as leader. Establishing objective accountability standards is a way of reiterating the convictions of the organization as a whole.

Now I would like to consider some effective *and* some ineffective ways to functionally use accountability in your business. Thus far we have tracked the purpose and value of accountability, but the difficult act of holding accountable is where most leaders fail.

Some leaders misuse accountability by constantly pointing out the failures of their employees, or ripping apart certain departments for their shortcomings at every meeting. These leaders usually meet the standards perfectly themselves, but have no mercy on those who fail to. They bang on the company, but do not build the company.

On the other extreme, we find leaders who are wishy-washy in their enforcement of standards, and who often have too much faith in their employees. Such leaders hold an "it will get done eventually" mindset, and usually fail to meet corporate standards themselves. Leaders of the first extreme are overly demanding and untrusting of their people; leaders of the second extreme demand too little, and barely hold their business accountable to anything at all. In my experience, these types of leaders lose their credibility within the organization over time. Employees may find their Boss Man a "nice guy," but because of his own failures to lead (and meet expectations), he will appear less and less like one to whom they must give account for their work.

Another accountability flop I often see is *inconsistency*. One meeting, the boss is yelling business standards and pointing out every flaw. Next meeting, the boss pushes problems "under the rug" and does not address performance issues in the company at all. They are inconsistent.

However, between the two extremes I have mentioned above is a balanced leader who knows how to use accountability effectively—in a way that actually improves the organization's alignment and moves it towards fulfilling a vision. This kind of leader embodies the standards of the business *for the business and the customers to see.* He or she is consistent in the way they hold the organization accountable. I have found that this usually requires a schedule of regular meetings and performance reviews on both the individual and departmental level (weekly, monthly, etc. but *stick to the schedule you set*). Use these times to examine what has been going right, and what needs improvement; use these times to hold your employees accountable. Further, a good leader knows to praise their employees for their work in public, and reprimand or critique for failures in private.

All of these means of holding your employees accountable to the standards of the company (and encouraging them to hold one another accountable) is a process of developing a language around performance. I cannot stress how important strong communication is when attempting to use accountability the right ways. Too many businesses suffer inner conflict from a simple lack of clarity about expectations. Because *accountability is the means by which you assure that everyone is doing what he or she is supposed to do*, clear communication is simply a must.

With a strong accountability system in place, I am convinced all the other efforts of your business will function more smoothly. Accountability is tied so tightly to the success of your business because it ensures and constantly checks on performance. Accountability allows you not only to ask, "how are we doing?" but also enables you to see how you're doing. Are we executing the strategy

ACCOUNTABILITY ALLOWS YOU NOT ONLY TO ASK, "HOW ARE WE DOING?" BUT ALSO ENABLES YOU TO SEE HOW YOU'RE DOING.

and moving towards the vision? Are these action plans aligned with the vision? Is this department doing what they should be? Accountability helps answer all these questions. And, in the end, it will show you why your company is generating the profit you need to, or why it's not. I hope you see how critical this is!

If you are a business leader or CEO reading this, I challenge you to step up and set the expectations for your business in both your words and actions. Use your platform to inform; use your position to set in motion the direction of your organization through accountability.

WHEN YOU THINK OF ACCOUNTABILITY, DO YOU THINK OF IT IN A NEGATIVE OR POSITIVE SENSE, AND WHY?

Question

2

ARE YOU ACCOUNTABLE (FOR ANYTHING) TO ANYONE RIGHT NOW?

Question

3

HOW ARE YOU LEVERAGING THE POWER OF ACCOUNTABILITY IN YOUR ORGANIZATION TODAY?

WHAT ARE THE DANGERS OF WRONGLY IMPLEMENTING ACCOUNTABILITY IN YOUR ORGANIZATION?

WHAT IS ONE ACTION YOU WILL TAKE IMMEDIATELY AS A RESULT OF READING THIS CHAPTER?

CHAPTER 7
SUCCESS

Success

Accountability

Alignment

Actions

Strategy

Vision

Leadership

"MOST PEOPLE **FAIL** IN LIFE NOT BECAUSE THEY AIM TOO HIGH AND MISS, BUT BECAUSE THEY **AIM TOO LOW AND HIT**."

Les Brown

CHAPTER 7

It is only fitting to wrap up this book with one word: Success.

The reason you will undergo any of the efforts of the previous chapters is to, in fact, *succeed*. It goes without saying, but the purpose of this book is to help you do just that: your vision, strategy, actions—everything—are meant to work *together* to help your business succeed in the areas it needs to. And I'm talking about your entire life here: professional, financial, relational, physical and spiritual. We all need motivation to stay the challenging courses of life and work; a proper understanding of success can offer us just that.

Success can be defined in two ways—one is hard and fast, the other is softer. The "hard" definition of success is the *simple accomplishment of an objective*. You made money; you purchased a bigger house; you obtained a new customer, etc. If your goal was to get a promotion, you succeed (according to this definition) when you actually *get the promotion*. It's simple, though not easy. On the other hand, the "soft" definition of success is the sense of mental and spiritual fulfillment that comes with achieving your goals. Here the emphasis is on your personal satisfaction with the work you've done and how you've contributed to something bigger than yourself. You are able to look back on it all and think *it was worth it*! Your efforts paid off, and thus, you obtain success.

It is quite possible to accomplish the first type of success—you get the promotion—without *feeling* that kind of fulfillment of the second definition. I want you to succeed in both ways, to climb the mountain and, from the top, see that all your hard work was worth it. Let's take a look at why a healthy understanding of success is so important for your organization and for your own life.

To begin, an understanding of success makes the road *to* success actually more enjoyable. Work, with a definite objective in mind, can feel less burdensome and more satisfying than work with no purpose. The mere thought of finally reaching your objective adds motivation to continue your striving towards it. Like we have discussed, as the leader of your business you must set the pace and the standards. This means you must be the one to keep sight of your goals; remember you are working towards success.

If you do *not* define and pursue success in your organization, work becomes trivial. In other words, you must answer the *why* before you answer the *how*. Without a sense of success, your business will work itself in circles—laboring day after day—without ever knowing if you have reached the goal. When will you be *done*? Every organization and every individual employee *needs* some sense of completion, of wholeness in terms of work. Otherwise, you are climbing a mountain with no peak, running a race with no finish line. On a personal level, we need success to know we have made some sort of difference. We need to know that our work matters—that we have improved, grown or accomplished something *successfully*.

I've explained why understanding success is so important, but how do we actually succeed? Or, how do we move from *wanting* success to *succeeding*? Here are some practical steps that will be helpful to you and your organization.

1. Track Your Progress

While working out your strategy every day, check often to see how effectively your business is moving towards attaining its vision. Don't just expect to be there by chance one day. As a leader, I find it helpful to keep a journal that tracks the attainment progress of my successes. This way, I can really gauge how I'm doing. Write down your goals and pay daily attention to the ways you are moving closer to, or further away from them. How are the action plans working to attaining your vision? Are you aligned in this department? Tracking progress is key.

2. Reward Small Successes

Having set an overarching vision for the organization, take some time to

SUCCESS

develop smaller objectives that boost confidence and morale along the way. After a busy holiday season, reward your leadership team with a small bonus—let them know they succeeded. If you are looking to lose 50 lbs. in a year, treat yourself to ice cream after a couple weeks of healthy eating and exercise. Reward small successes as you move towards your ultimate objective.

3. Stay The Course

With a clear vision of what you want to do, a definite game plan, and with the proper resources and accountability in place, *commit yourself.* In the end, the grand majority of individuals and organizations fail to truly succeed because they cannot commit when the going gets tough. But we should expect the going to get tough! This is precisely when you need to stay the course you've chosen. Trust in all of the planning and brainstorming work you've done up to this point. Trust in your leadership teams. Forget about excuses; stick to what you said you were going to do! As the saying goes, quitters never win and winners never quit. Stay the course and you will succeed.

No matter the current circumstances of your organization, I want to encourage you to set great goals—to dream BIG. Likewise, to those of you who are reading this while planning to start a new business: do not be afraid to make plans that might seem intimidating. I want you to pursue success as something that is extremely attainable. Because, with the right steps and planning, *it is!* Let this motivate you and your organization to pursue success through excellence every day, rather than working in frustrating circles to no end.

As individuals, we are too often discouraged by the doubtful judgments of others around us—those who see our dreams and scoff. They are likely skeptical about our success because they themselves were too afraid to commit to big dreams. But you *can* commit. Whether you are at the base of the mountain, or half way up, always keep the peak in mind. Look forward to reaching your objectives and having the satisfaction to look back at all the planning and work you executed to get there. Take pride in what you have done and have faith in what you can do.

In my experience, reaching success is never truly the end—because success will always continue to motivate. If you accomplish your first climb of 500 ft., it will likely drive you to a new challenge, a new vision: 1,000 ft.,

93

10,000 ft., and beyond. Success engenders more success. It will give you the confidence to set bigger and better objectives. Thus, as you can see, a proper understanding of success is critical for the growth of your business, just as it is critical to your growth as a business leader. Yes, attaining success is hard, but it is an adventure worth taking. And I am confident it is one you are now prepared to take!

So, I want to leave you with two final thoughts.

The first one is a big one. Think of this: you and I are both going to reach our final hour. That's right, we are all terminal—we are going to die. Our culture does a great job at hiding death, but I think there's a reason why the richest man to ever live said, "It is better to spend your time at funerals than at festivals. For you are going to die, and you should think about it while there is still time."

> ## THAT'S RIGHT, WE ARE ALL TERMINAL —WE ARE GOING TO DIE.

Wow.

Why would I end this book and the chapter on Success by talking about death? Well, I think there is certainly some merit to what Mel Gibson's character William Wallace uttered in the classic movie *Braveheart* when he proclaimed that all men die, but few men ever truly live.

My friend, achieving success is easy but leaving a legacy is something altogether different. How I measure success today should be in alignment with how I will measure success on my deathbed. I'm not going to wish I had worked more or labored harder as much as I will think about *who* I dedicated my life to—*who* I spent my time with and how I added value to their lives in a way that will impact generations to come.

> ## MY FRIEND, ACHIEVING SUCCESS IS EASY BUT LEAVING A LEGACY IS SOMETHING ALTOGETHER DIFFERENT.

Don't get me wrong, I want to work hard each and every day that I step into my office. But I also want to know that my wife knows I will love her until the day I die—her and no other. I want my family to know that they and God were the single biggest driving forces of my life. I don't want them to have a shadow of a doubt about that absolute fact. Otherwise, what's the point? What am I going to take with me when I leave? That's what matters. That's how I measure success, and I want to encourage you to live every day with your Vision in mind. But, don't forget what's truly, truly important. Now, *and* at that final hour we will all inevitably come to.

Don't try to do it all at once, just take it one day at a time—one action at a time and 1% at a time. …Which is the final thought: just get 1% better every day. Not 100% better, but just one. If you get 1% better every day for a year—well, you can do the math.

So this is where I leave you and where I call you out. Each and every day, how are you going to be a 1% better leader, husband/wife, father/mother, etc? I know you can do it, and I am here to help. So get this thing done. This book ends where we started—with you. In the words of the late and great Dr. Robert H. Schuller, "If it's going to be, it's up to me."

HOW CAN I PERSONALLY HELP YOU ACHIEVE YOUR SUCCESS? REALLY, I WANT TO KNOW. EMAIL ME AT CHUCK@TOMCAT-GROUP.COM

Question

2

HOW ARE YOU GOING TO BE 1% BETTER TODAY?

HOW ARE YOU GOING TO DEFINE SUCCESS FROM THIS DAY FORWARD?

Question

4

WHAT WORDS WOULD DESCRIBE THE LEGACY YOU'VE BEEN LEAVING UP TO THIS POINT IN YOUR LIFE?

WHAT ARE THE WORDS THAT WILL DESCRIBE THE LEGACY YOU WILL LEAVE FROM THIS DAY FORWARD?

ABOUT THE AUTHOR

CHUCK GUMBERT

WEBSITE:
ChuckGumbert.com

LINKEDIN:
linkedin.com/in/chuckgumbert

EMAIL:
chuck@tomcat-group.com

CHUCK GUMBERT, The Turnaround Specialist™, has utilized a wealth of life and business experience, as well as a knack for overcoming challenges, to guide numerous clients to success. One of Chuck's first major challenges—overcoming the debilitating effects of polio at age 2—did not stop him from eventually participating in high school athletics and later becoming a fighter pilot in the U.S. Navy, graduating at the top of his class. His drive for accomplishment led to him climbing Mt. Kilimanjaro and becoming a nationally recognized business leader, entrepreneur, speaker and mentor.

Chuck has been heavily influenced by historic leaders in both business and the military—most notably motivational speaker Zig Ziglar, editor of Success Magazine Darren Hardy, business leader, author and speaker Jeff Hayzlett, Vietnam POW Captain John M. McGrath USN Ret. and General George S. Patton.

Chuck has applied his core principles and proven Success Model in the business world, advising corporate leaders and their teams how to achieve predictable and consistent success. A true leader in an ever-changing America, Chuck is known for his high integrity, pristine character, drive and ability to "get the job done" - no matter what the circumstances. He has the unique ability to quickly diagnosis complicated problems and breakdowns within an organization, rally the troops to get everyone on board working towards a common goal and launch a solid success strategy for improved and accelerated performance.

Chuck's demonstrated success includes:
Executive Leadership
Strategy Development and Implementation
Organizational Alignment and Accountability

Turnarounds / Transformations
Improved Operational Performance
Business Growth

Chuck's business experience includes:
CEO, President, Vice President/General Manager, Director
Interim Executive Leadership
Business Advisor
Acquisition Integration
Operations Leader
Business Development
New Manufacturing and Aftermarket Activities
Multi-Site Management
'Fast Track' New Product Introduction
FAA Part 145, 135
AS9100

Chuck's industry experience includes:
Aircraft Structures Machining and Assembly
Turbine Engines & Component Repairs
Aircraft Maintenance & Conversions
Electromechanical Components
Instruments & Avionics
HIT & IGT Components
Telemetry and Data Link Antenna Systems
Oil & Gas Pipeline/Station Construction and Maintenance
Civic Events

Chuck's education includes:
University of Texas at Arlington - BBA
Six Sigma - GE Engine Services
Theory of Constraints - Goldratt Institute
Critical Chain - Goldratt Institute
Strategic Leadership - Center for Creative Leadership

FOR A **COMPLIMENTARY** 30 MINUTE CONSULTATION, CONTACT CHUCK:

(210) 262-5880
CHUCK@TOMCAT-GROUP.COM